THE SHUTTERS

THE SHUTTERS

AHMED BOUANANI

Translated from the French by Emma Ramadan

A New Directions Paperbook Original

The Shutters was originally published in Morocco as *Les Persiennes* (1980) by Éditions Stouky. *Photograms* was originally published in France as *Photogrammes* (1989) by Éditions Avant-Quart.

Manufactured in the United States of America
New Directions Books are printed on acid-free paper
First published as a New Directions Paperbook (NDP1410) in 2018

Library of Congress Cataloging-in-Publication Data
Names: Bouanani, Ahmed author. | Ramadan, Emma translator.
Title: The shutters / by Ahmed Bouanani; translated from the French by Emma Ramadan.
Other titles: Persiennes. English
Description: New York : New Directions Publishing, 2018.
Identifiers: LCCN 2018009101 (print) | LCCN 2018002149 (ebook) | ISBN 9780811227858 () | ISBN 9780811227841 (alk. paper)
Classification: LCC PQ3989.2.B629 (print) | LCC PQ3989.2.B629 P413 2018 (ebook) | DDC 848/.91409—dc23
LC record available at https://lccn.loc.gov/2018009101

10 9 8 7 6 5 4 3 2 1

New Directions Books are published for James Laughlin
by New Directions Publishing Corporation
80 Eighth Avenue, New York 10011
ndbooks.com

Contents

Translator's Foreword

The Shutters is a book made out of memories. It insists on remembering, on telling stories of Morocco's history so that the past isn't pushed into obscurity. Its author, Ahmed Bouanani, was born in Casablanca in 1938. Through a mix of prose, prose poems, free and rhymed verse, Bouanani claws and scrapes through his country's collective memory, reconstructing vivid pictures of Morocco's past by intertwining legend and tradition with the familiar surroundings of his present. At the heart of the book stands the house with the shutters—the house where the narrator lives with his grandmother, and where his ancestors, along with a number of legendary figures, from Scheherazade to the horse-woman Al-Buraq, pass through.

While *The Shutters* contains references to the Second World War, the Rif War, and the Spanish and French protectorates, what is perhaps most palpable of all is the violence inflicted on Morocco by its own government during the period known as *les années de plomb*—the years of lead. Following Moroccan independence from the French in 1956, it became obvious to many artists and intellectuals that the battle for a liberated Morocco had only just begun. The generation that had seen its national culture wiped out by the French protectorate then saw it denied, or confined to the realm of folklore, by the post-independence government as a way to keep the Moroccan people from uniting with anything resembling national pride. The palace took back all power; no democratic principles were instated; leftist parties were outlawed and harassed. The government assumed more control over its people through the Arabization of the education system, effectively cutting off the younger generation from any Western thought. King Hassan II persecuted democratic and progressive thinking with torture and imprisonment. In Bouanani's pages, dead soldiers, prisoners, and poets scream in their tombs with their mouths full of dirt.

As the violence and turmoil continued, living traditions were slowly erased. And if the past disappears, how can one construct a future? Bouanani believed that tradition held the keys to a country's identity. He dedicated his life to digging through his country's buried past, upholding myth over official history, and plunging into the void to bring back a vibrant heritage that was forgotten but not annihilated. He did not want to imitate what came before colonization, but instead wanted to rediscover Morocco's national heritage and critically reinvent it, something at once anchored in the ancient, in popular and oral traditions, and also infused with the new.

Many intellectuals in the 1960s and '70s decided to fight back through the written word. Early on, Ahmed Bouanani was part of the group of writers involved with the literary journal *Souffles*, founded by Abdellatif Laâbi and Mostafa Nissabouri. Through their journal they stressed the importance of culture in bringing about political change, the idea that through the celebration of Moroccan traditions, people could forge a stronger sense of communal identity. Bouanani published an extremely nuanced essay on oral poetry and wrote a history of Moroccan cinema. He played an active role in the Marrakech Popular Arts Festival, and made detailed drawings of Berber jewelry. In 1971, after a seven-year run, *Souffles* was forced to shut down; many of its principal members were arrested and tortured, while others fled the country. These individuals are the poet-prisoners of the collection *Les Persiennes* (*The Shutters*).

Create, build, rebuild on the disappearing ruins of former days. Bouanani's poetry collection *Photogrammes* (*Photograms*), also included in this volume, embodies this idea as well. He plays with classical verse forms, making unusual turns of phrase and inserting rhymes in unexpected places, or sometimes abruptly abandoning the rhyme scheme altogether. Gruesome scenes, graphic descriptions, swear words, denouncements, rage all feed into the playful lines, further heightening the contrast with the sad scenes of poverty and oppression. The poet rebels against classical forms by using them to express taboo themes. Unruly punctuation, surreal imagery, sudden tense shifts, and an always-morphing format also play into the experience of reading Bouanani's poems on his own terms.

The great Moroccan author Mohammed Khaïr-Eddine said that Bouanani's poems "invigorate a dying Maghrebi literature, which is taking refuge more and more in the fantasies of the West." His poetry bears the imprint of colonization's violence, and is written in an imposed language with a "strange alphabet." Bouanani evokes his hometown Casablanca, the odors of mats and mosques, the fear of famine, the minarets "planted in our flesh," as a way to keep his "memory intact ... / the places—the names—the actions—our voices." In "The Illiterate Man," the narrator's father goes insane after reading the books left behind by his ancestors. His sanity returns only after he has used an ax to smash into pieces the chest in which the books were stored.

Ahmed Bouanani, though a prolific writer, was hesitant to publish any of his work, and was known primarily as a filmmaker during his lifetime. He directed four short films: *Les quatre sources*, *Tarfaya ou La marche d'un poète*, *Six et douze* (shot in Casablanca from 6:00 a.m. to noon), and *Mémoire 14*, which was censored from a full-length film to twenty-four minutes due to its use of archival images and footage from the Rif War. Bouanani also directed a feature-length film *Le Mirage* about a poor man in the 1940s who finds a stack of money in a sack of flour, which then leads him on a search for traces of collective memory in a place without any frames of reference, images of the Moroccan people's history montaged with a French-imposed modernity. Whether through films or through books, Bouanani's goal was always the same: to dive into his country's suppressed past through the lens of the present moment.

The written work Bouanani decided to publish in his lifetime comprises three volumes of poetry—*The Shutters, Photograms*, and the yet-to-be translated *Territoire de l'instant* (Land of the moment)—as well as one novel, *L'hôpital* (*The Hospital*), a hallucinatory tale in which the hospital patients turn into prisoners. Almost as soon as the novel was published in 1990 it disappeared. Over two decades later, it was reissued in both Morocco and France to international acclaim. When Bouanani passed away in Demnate, Morocco, in 2011, he left behind a daughter, Touda Bouanani, and boxes full of unpublished manuscripts stacked in his old apartment in Rabat. In the years since her father's death, Touda has rescued these works from a devastating fire and has been making great efforts to bring his unpublished and out-of-print texts into the public light. There are notebooks, journals, essays, translations, poems, short stories, a trilogy of novels, screenplays, and many drawings still awaiting publication. Even with Touda's progress, the vast majority of his oeuvre still awaits discovery.

I received a Fulbright fellowship to Morocco in 2014 to study and translate Bouanani's work, and to help organize the incredible treasure trove of his archives. I worked alongside Touda and Omar Berrada at the Dar al-Ma'mûn artist residency, adding to the years of work they had already done to promote Bouanani's films and books, while trying to bring some of his unpublished writing into the public light. At the Dar al-Ma'mûn library, I had access to books about Moroccan history and culture, as well as books written by Bouanani's contemporaries about the political climate of their day, all of which served as necessary references in translating his poetry.

For Ahmed Bouanani, to write was to witness, to save tradition from oblivion, to wrest a people from submission. As he once wrote, "These memories retrace the seasons of a country that was quickly forgetful of its past, indifferent to its present, constantly turning its back on its future." Now, I am excited to finally share these powerful poems with the English-speaking world—poems that boldly remember in order to face the future. Thank you to Touda Bouanani, Omar Berrada, Juan Asís Palao Gómez, and the countless others working on Ahmed Bouanani's archives, for their time and help on this project during my stay in Morocco, and for their continued support.

—EMMA RAMADAN

THE SHUTTERS

The Shutters

In days past, when the world was inhabited by giants, and every Friday the ocean drained the dead fish and octopi onto the sand, I had a name, an age, I answered "present," I sketched figures on graph paper, figures and movements, uniform silhouettes, trembling structures that always gave rise to minuscule continents, cataclysms overflowing the red margin.

I was a black fish, my head heavier, bigger, a body that was frail, burned, and dreams atop bicycles, dreams as big as the palm of a hand, would die at dawn, spreading all around my body beneath the sheets in the damp sunlight. Every time I felt them die the same death at the foot of a cliff in an eternal fall.

My first years were spent behind the shutters, in a room without engravings, in the silence of a thousand-year-old archaeology invariably disturbed every morning at the hour of the swallows and the distant bugles of the barracks at the edge of the forest, by the heavy and terrifying screeching of the hearses ...

1

These were long nights, never-ending nights when the world beyond the shutters swung toward the savage countries, toward insurrection and wars. The sky was never filled with stars but with deep, ancient voices that spoke to me in a monotone, often making me grab hold of my bedsheets with clammy, trembling hands.

I lived in a house as big as a dream you don't wake up from. Sometimes, when I was on the terrace of that house, giants wearing glasses would approach me. They would shake my hand with kindness, and tell me the story of a universe where the rivers and streams sweep along waves of milk and honey. Each time they finished their story, I would see a ball of fire fall on the sleeping city.

Someone is dead, they said.
God wasted Satan-the-thrice-damned.
A flower has wilted in paradise.
Someone is dead, they said, and no matter how tightly my hands gripped the bedsheets, the deep, ancient voices would weigh on my skull for never-ending nights.

2

Warped dreams, in the hangman's mask, started slipping beneath my shirt, day and night. They spawned beasts of many heads, like screaming children. At the same time, everywhere on the sidewalks, at the foot of the walls, in front of bus stations, police stations, mosques harboring stinkbugs reeking of humans in the mats' braids, and the barracks where the cruel soldiers were all too eager to laugh while devouring their chocolate bars, the hordes of leprous beggars had come to invade the city only to die at daybreak.

The screeching of the city's hearses, I heard it every day upon waking. Once, a hearse passed very close to the shutters. It carried off Yetto the old woman who had already lost her lips and fingers. They covered her body with a burlap sack, they washed the few cobblestones that had been her home with large buckets of water. Dead, she had become suddenly small, the size of a child. One day, I asked Grandmother Yamna where all the city's dead were buried. She replied that they hadn't been buried, the dead of those years. Some were thrown to the animals of the Aïn Sebaâ Zoo, and the rest they turned into cakes sold by peddlers on the Day of Ashura, the festival of mourning.

3

Grandmother Yamna was the strangest being in the house of the shutters. She was known throughout the neighborhood for her talismans that guarded against measles and trachoma. She deciphered the most difficult dreams, the ones where white horsemen emerged from clouds, just before dawn, or others that were even stranger, where the dead, resurrected, returned to keep the living company. She says that she was born under Moulay Al Hassan, during the terrible exodus of her family, chased from their land by the defeat. She also says that her half-brother was killed in an ambush one night in the month of Rajab ... He slumped over his horse, and his mother Deda Aïcha gathered him in her arms and drank the blood from his wound ...

Before the arrival of Milouda of Rehamna, it was Grandmother who carried me on her back. She was the first to wake up in the house of the shutters. Every morning at seven o'clock (deep, ancient voices seemed to spring at that moment from the windows of Derb Chorfa), dreams skittered like little insects over my chest and, before she placed me on her back, they would all hide in my hair.

4

On rainy mornings, the salty odor of the ocean infiltrated the houses with its stench of seaweed and fish. The swallows, always celebrating, amused themselves with dizzying swerves from the power lines. When they stole the yellow babouches of fkih Si Najem, teacher of Islamic law, they felt the fires of hell in his curses, which followed the screeching birds for an entire morning, up to the slums of Ben M'sik where, seemingly, the swallows transformed into kids dressed in rags.

5

Grandmother Yamna would hand me over to fkih Si Najem. In class, there were fifty children subjected to the same fate. For never-ending hours, the Prophet and his Companions sat among us directly upon the ground. The sky and the earth multiplied by seven, Yajouz and Mayajouz dug the labyrinths of the world with their fingers, Dejjal the Blind Liar roasted lambs and fish in the sun's face, and the monstrous Debba with the hair of a goat was born in the Souss and hurried to our class to choose her victims from among the young children who straddled flies and landed unbeknownst to anyone on fkih Si Najem's swollen nose.

6

When I returned to the house with the shutters, I would hide on the terrace. From there I observed the city and the somber clouds that transformed constantly beneath my gaze. I imagined titanic duels between horses of light and mile-long birds, their torn-out feathers suddenly changing into pieces of human flesh, the great wind sweeping the frenzied crowds far away, very far away toward less familiar horizons. Sometimes, for no apparent reason, I would cry, I would tell myself that the entire world was dead, that the house with the shutters would one day be destroyed by those immense

American balloons that often flew over the city. I would wake up with a start, in the middle of the night, and the deep, ancient voices (they would come from the hall) would grab me by the hair. Then I would tell myself that the end of the world was near, that it would happen when all the children were seated listening to fkih Si Najem talk about the scale that weighs pieces of human flesh.

7

Si Ben Alila, with his yellow gaze and his implicit murmurs, I see him again with my father surrounded by pale afternoons. With a satisfied, solemn air, he unfolds the roll of paper hidden somewhere beneath his black burnoose and he begins to read the never-ending list of ancestors in an apocalyptic voice.

From this dense text, words that seemed to live the life of silent, secret plants occupied even the smallest corner of the room, unknown generations emerging from centuries of furor and blood. Old men with incredibly long beards would sit on the mat in front of me, leaning on pillows or climbing the walls with sinister cracks of their vertebrae. They drowned themselves in diaphanous and vaporous colors when Si Ben Alila called out their names. An entire world of sheepskins stinking of camphor, the stenches of the Orient, and the brackish ink of Quranic schools, of lives filled with wisdom, of proverbs and prayers, of female and male saints, of lords helmeted with metal and shielded with blessings reborn on the battlefield or in peaceful lessons, surrounded by books and progeny. In the space of a silence, of a barely audible word, of a trembling sigh, time would sweep away the palaces and the houses, wrinkles would spread across faces, swords would rust in chests, women would sell harnesses while plunged in mourning, and children, now old, would look back on their tragedies, and all the ancient glories would disappear in the depths of ruins and storms. Dawn would rise again on a brighter world, a world less gleaming with emeralds. The yellow words would reveal other tragedies, bloody ambushes. My grandfather would stand up, smiling, and look at me. No birth. A life made of champing horses and Mokahlas encrusted with precious stones and Hassani and Portuguese coins. He would vigorously climb the forty steps of the house with the shutters, lift me up by the armpits, puff up his hairy cheeks, and blow like a happy devil. When he died no one in the house cried. My father, returning from the funeral, withdrew to his room and closed the door without a sound. It wasn't until later, much later, that I heard Grandmother arguing endlessly about my grandfather's savings and the missing crate. She would shake her head and keep repeating that all the saints of paradise, now deaf and blind, had long ago turned their backs on all that happened on earth.

8

The water sold at the cemetery every Friday always smells like tar. My mother and Grandmother Yamna especially think that God, on this day, allows his dead to return to the earth to listen to the orations and tally the family members who have come to mourn them. Their souls hide in the shells of insects, in the petals of flowers growing out of tombs. The soul of my grandfather was happy. It was a multicolored butterfly that fluttered about with the same energy as when he was alive, and had it not been unable to speak, it would have congratulated me for reciting a long verse of the Quran in his memory without making a single mistake.

One very hot day, in the early afternoon, a man knocked on the door of the house with the shutters. When I opened the door, he lifted me up from the ground and kissed me on both cheeks. He shoved me into his spiky neckbeard and asked me if I recognized him. Then he put me down and paused for a long moment at the threshold, not knowing if he should stay or go. It's true, he said, you couldn't possibly recognize me. When I left you were no bigger than this! And he showed me his thumb. My mother, seeing him, cried out as if she had just seen a rat emerge from behind the vase, and then said: My God, if she saw you looking like this!

She saw him. With a bucketful of water in her hand, Grandmother had climbed the forty steps, cursing all the staircases of the city, and shouted when she saw him: M'hammed, my son! She took him in her arms, kissed him on the beard, released him from her embrace, and dealt him a magisterial smack on the cheek: That's for abandoning your mother, you degenerate! How dare you return after being gone for so many years?

The very next day, Grandmother set about finding him a wife. Very soon after, she found him a suitable woman. Uncle M'hammed accepted the introduction. They went together straight away to pay her a courtesy call. When Grandmother came back, she announced that Uncle M'hammed was married. Over the second cup of tea he had decided to marry Lalla Hnia. He had barely murmured a few reflections on her age when Grandmother energetically intervened. She didn't leave until after the Adouls arrived and a marriage contract had been drawn up. Not even one week had passed before Lalla Hnia burst into the house with the shutters, loudly demanding a large silver tray, two wool blankets, a silk belt, and some jewels that M'hammed-the-wretched had been sure to grab before taking off without leaving an address. He wouldn't return until many years later, a little bitter, exhausted from a long journey on foot that had taken him to the vineyards of Oranie. When he married Hachmia, his sixth and final wife, he was already no more than a shadow of himself. Even today, sometimes he remembers. And then he lashes out at his wife, at the objects that surround him in the little shack, objects that never change.

10

Time stops, a piece of newspaper remains. A tale is assassinated at the foot of a tree, and all travelers avoid it. They pass far from the ford where gold burns.

A grandmother remembers the fair season, the leprous horsemen, the dragons with manes falling from the moon ... A star licks its fingers, a child on a terrace throws the sun a rotten tooth. The child learns the magic words:

> Little sun, take this donkey's tooth
> And give me the tooth of a gazelle!

Little sun, take. Three times. The rays absorb the tooth, the magic words at the speed of light. A cut from a razor on his right thigh, Tarras Boulba jumps from a wagon howling like an Apache. Forty steps in the house with the shutters—go up them on your head and the world flips upside down.

But then who looked at themselves in the ringed mirror, seeking their own brutal death?

Near the hairdresser's, Abdallah-Al-Aariane secretly sells kif he stashes in a hidden drawer under his stool, safe from the eyes of the police. Bousbir's tenants chew gum and hum Egyptian songs. Kids collect trash from the stream at Derb Al Kabir and hastily draw swastikas on the sidewalk. In the Houfra neighborhood, fire-fighters pull the cadaver of a woman who committed suicide from a well, while at Yafelmane, near the Cinéma Royal, people sing a song of the ancient Far West to the rhythm of a tin-can guembri. Little Soldier Ahmed wears the shoes of a former combatant, he feasts with his eyes on Superman in front of the Cinéma Bahia where a police officer whips the crowd squabbling around the cash register. When we were eight years old we reenacted the two wars, we embarked on crusades, we swore we'd destroy all the slums. At Ben M'sik, at Ould Aïcha, at the Carrières Centrales, every day there were new barracks and minarets patched with the winged horse of Mobiloil. When we were eight years old we left for Hiroshima, for Indochina. We were done with the bands of Derb Al Kabir, with the bands of the Spagnol and Baladia neighborhoods. The Moroccan soldiers died for a fistful of rice, it was written on their tombs. Only the French died for France. When Khammar returned from World War II, all he had left was one leg and a lot of medals. The Germans were over there, and I, fifty yards away, turned myself over to Moulay Abdelkader Jilali, I pulled the trigger, mowing down a hundred Germans like wheat, I pulled again, another hundred, an entire battalion dead, and I was left alone, my companions killed in the ambush. My right leg? I had to abandon it on the battlefield because it got in my way.

War was revived in every neighborhood. Hitler died hundreds of times each day. An entire cataclysmic world knocked at our doors. The house with the shutters stood firm. Its forty steps led to the seventh heaven where the giants wore glasses.

11

Our world felt the war. We feared famine, and then it came. Dead bodies lay in front of the grain market, in front of the barracks of chocolate. When the American soldiers passed through the neighborhood, there was widespread pandemonium. *Okay, come on boys!* The kids grabbed onto the trucks. Even the elderly held out their hands. Tarras Boulba almost fell backward. His hands dripped with chocolate. He pirouetted away and hid in a back alley to devour the skin of his hand in peace.

12

A time. A possible fragment of time.

A phonograph tells the story of the city dweller who was fooled by the country bumpkin. Oum Kalthoum playing Dananir and Smahane on the sun's hair. The phonograph explodes. The war continues. A web of maimed legends. The photograph never stops smiling. And Driss is dead. Dead. Driss Ben M'hammed ben Salah ben. Dead. Not the war. Tuberculosis. Flies on his face. No more smile. No more uniform. The barrack reeks of death. Lips can no longer speak. Swollen. They murmur. Death takes him by the toes. They turn icy cold. A door opened over there, Grandmother said. The web has come undone. Is sewn back up. Is sewn back up like a knife wound.

13

Grandmother sings. She sings on the terrace of the house with the shutters. Heart full of death, cheeks bloodied.

One day my hair will be white.
Her hair white, she says: I will cry all the tears in my body.

In his song God was magnanimous and his pity deep as a well.

Will my liver ever leave me in peace?

Grandmother sings. In the sky of Derb Tolba a gigantic balloon full of green spiders passes by.

The house with the shutters will long remember the bomb that cracked the facade.

The bomb where later we'll put plastic flowers.

14

Countless birds died on the terraces. We made meatballs out of them, we ate them in a corner, we passed the time making traps. Imagined death. Designed death. Circle of wire. Then the locusts crashed down onto the city. If I could remember the days. Remember the days. The circle of wire. Expanded. Diamond. Triangle. It was cold. No. Brackish sky. Fish guts abandoned on the beach. My memory: a kick from the donkey that passed, carrying manure.

Five francs. Five francs per kilo of grilled locusts. Come on, good people, there aren't many left. Taste this, little one, isn't it tasty as a chicken leg? Five francs. Only five francs, come on Muslims. Then the locusts stopped coming from Sudan. My memory: a kick from the donkey. A song builds. Ragged. Hands gray from cold. Built. Gesticulated. Small lips of starving neighborhoods.

> Salted locust
> Where were you then?
>
> In your grandmother's gardens
>
> And what did you eat?
> And what did you drink in my grandmother's gardens?
>
> Only apples
> only nectar

In the photographs. The street.
In the shredded liver of Grandmother Yamna.
The song that forgives the song
that is sewn back up
    was sewn back up
        like a knife wound.

15

More swallows land on the telephone wires. They come down in the latest renditions of a dreamed fall at dawn. The deep, mono-tone voices shatter. Beyond the house with the shutters, a new light settles over the city, chasing the ogress with her breasts slung over her shoulders and the last nursery rhymes murmured in front of secondhand clothing stores. Silence. Silence in my past. The skull feeds. No more war. No more screams. No more hearses. A star sings. The star does not sing. It's a kid from Derb Spagnol. One of the band. He sings at the top of his lungs as the morning bicyclists pass.

If Madame comes
we will give her ragout
if Monsieur comes
we will give him couscous
if their son comes
we will slit his throat and say nothing.

In the house with the shutters, voices.

The Quran. And my mother, and my father in front of the ringed mirror. A smell of Brazilian coffee. Smell of winter. A breeze in the leaves of an unknown tree. Milouda captured in the light. The red of her skirt—or her hands—a red that spreads the legs and shows her genitals. Look. A copper pestle. Big as an arm. Milouda sits on the ground and she spreads her legs. Near the door, to avoid Grandmother Yamna when she emerges from the terrace where she does her ablutions. The copper sparkles in the prism of light. The wound opens slightly. Swallows the pestle little by little. And Milouda laughs. A long time ago, she cried. In the middle of a big bloodstain. Grandmother shook her head, protested. Brandishing Milouda's bloody sirwal. And Milouda laughs. Her big lips spread open. Look. The pestle sparkles in the light. Come. She says. Don't be afraid, look, we ... Silence. The skull feasts. More songs come through the telephone wires. As the morning bicyclists pass. The lament, "freshwater, freshwater" as the morning bicyclists pass captured in the light of bygone days.

The baker El Miseria worked for Monsieur Gauthier. Bread all day. That's not a life, Master Hammou. To bake bread twenty-four hours a day and earn barely enough to feed the kids ...! There were nine of them. The older one gathered junk at the American depot in Ben M'sik. One day I'll go to Europe. He unzipped his fly, grabbed his penis, and daydreamed. Golden canopy beds. White sheets. Red lips. Blonde hair. His dream explodes over the trash. El Miseria: to bake bread twenty-four hours a day and earn barely enough to ... There were nine of them, they looked at the sawhorse with three planks and didn't understand a thing. Didn't understand how death entered the bakery. The older child took over for his father. Baked bread for Monsieur Gauthier twenty-four hours a day. You see, it's the heat that killed my father. Soon, he says: That's not a life, son of my master. To bake bread twenty-four hours a day and earn barely enough to ... There were twelve of them. The older child took over for the father. And he got married, not even seventeen years old. His young wife kept giving birth. She makes babies and I make bread. Aïe, madre mia, they don't need to recruit soldiers, they can just enlist my entire family ... Perhaps the dream retained a fragrance of a faraway land, of trash from the American depot.

17

Freshwater, freshwater.

At the passing of the morning bicyclists captured in the light, a face is born. Face of a little adventure that lasted the span of a wink behind the shutters. Eight years. Me, twelve, maybe. She never went out. To make a talisman, you need a thousand francs. Why not try the date? But how to get one of the girl's hairs? Without the hair, the date is useless. And so, and so, she moved. One morning, the shutters opened. Painters came to whitewash the room that had been closed for a long time. Other tenants. Algerians. They spoke French. Without an accent. Their son. No more name. Or age. Spoke of a faraway country inhabited by Christians. New furniture. A lot of money. Of snow. Of golden curls. Of bulldogs wearing sweaters. One day, he showed me one, in the ancient medina. It was dressed like a gentleman, and scampered about on the heels of an old woman shading herself from the sun with a scarlet umbrella. She looked like an oak tree. It was the first time I saw a dog dressed better than a boy from our part of town. I went out other times with the son of the new tenants. He told me about Oran, Mostaganem, other cities. He looked at the sky. The clouds coming from far away. Like fishermen's barges. Their son. No more name. The same age. A little body with skinny legs. Hair black and smooth like mine. Eyes. His eyes blur. Fade. His hands too. The little body crushed on the sidewalk. The little pool of blood . . .

In the country of memory
a fistful of suns
tiny fingers dreaming of chocolate
cinemas stinking of cresyl and the rainforest
Tarzan and Fu Manchu Robin Hood and Frankenstein
the phantom of the opera . . . in the country of memory
the heart that doesn't stop
crying
    or laughing
        or jumping rope.

A bird in the mortar. Spring passes on a turtle's back. And the wind blows, ripping out all the flowers in the world. My aunt takes off her djellaba, her veil, and her babouches. Puts her index finger on her lips, complains of the ingratitude of her nephews and nieces. For hours. She calls me "big head." She cries, she laughs, we tickle her, she howls. She mistakes a belt for a snake. Swears to never step foot in the house again. Tells a story about a reptile numb with cold. The sun descends behind her back. For a moment it remains suspended at her shoulders. And abruptly my aunt ages a few years, and the tears that run down her wrinkled cheeks seem to take on the color of summer.

19

In the night, a tomcat meowed for a mate. He hid behind a car. Screechings. The horror of a child on his way to be slaughtered by the butcher's knife. I heard the deep, monotone voices announcing cataclysms and nightmares. The street went on and on. There was a clinic at the end of it. No, the clinic hadn't been built yet. Stable, manure. Bare feet smeared with feces. A liter, two liters of milk. For … Only his voice can still be heard. He once knew a time when the Italians reigned over Morocco. Then the Germans came and they burned the Jews in the Mellah. Not long after, the Americans, the candy, the chewing gum, the chocolate bars, the nuclear bases, work, horrible accidents, pieces of human flesh sliced up with a blowtorch. My uncle Allal. Allal ben M'hammed ben. Scuba diver. Finally, he buys a bicycle. Drinks red wine until he pukes it up, prays when he can, and beats his wife every night. So, the French …

Each man in the neighborhood had a personal history with the country. Grandmother Yamna sighs. It was long before you were born, a long time ago. I was still a young girl and I don't remember which sultan was reigning then: perhaps Moulay Hassan or Moulay Abd El Aziz or Moulay Hafid. In any event, one of them was in the Fes palace at the time. The people prayed in his name and paid the tertib tax in his name, too. When the rumor spread that the country had been invaded, a mad fear took hold of us. We wondered what the Christians looked like, and we talked nonstop about the Beni-Kalbouns and the Beni-Ara, but no one had seen them, not even at Ben Guerir. Everywhere, we got ready to fight the invaders that had come to devour our children and spread Satan's religion ... how many years ago was that now? Can you tell me? Look in your book. And when I consult my History book and reply, she looks at me, grimaces, and asks me how I'm able to know all these things about the past if I was born only yesterday.

20

A public garden at night. Centuries of light above us. The city trembled in our flesh. A long time ago ... A bicycle passed. A drunkard. Two guards whacked him hard on the head. His nose bled, his eyes were crazed. He stunk of grain alcohol. Once again silence. Night. You weren't looking at me. I didn't know you would die soon. A ridiculous death, like indigestion.
"Life is good, no?"
"Yes, very good."
"So why do they keep us from living it?"
    The city trembled in our flesh. We were young or old, it doesn't matter. We fervently desired insane things, insane dreams, we

devoured the city in our imagination. In our imagination, we drank from every spring, hurtled down every mountain, crossed every ocean, every land, every capital, conquered every star. Shoeless, we had both entered into an eternity fixed like death.

And like the autumn trees
we had suddenly
lost
all our leaves.

21

There were no more swallows on the telephone wires. The light no longer played in the palm of my hand. The crowd on the sidewalk. Around a red circle. At eight in the morning. Eight fifteen in the morning. January of . . . Already twelve years ago. The cup of coffee was still hot. It stays hot in my memory. A past in the newspaper or a litany of ancient photographs. Someone had grabbed his 7.65mm revolver hidden in a pile of mint. He grabbed his revolver hidden in a pile of mint. Only one bullet, tiny. He fires the only bullet, one bullet is enough. And the sun felt dizzy. Morning no longer knows which way to turn. The entire city, the walls, the lights, the new sky where the stars barely had time to turn on. Everything falls in front of my bicycle. Collapses. A police officer stops me. No, let him go, it's his dad. It's my dad. And the entire city says that it's my dad. Death's memory endures. Red boots on the cold sidewalk. A red trickle on a forehead. Already, already . . . The ambulance goes through my body. The telephone wires go through my body. I die to be born a second time. On a bigger bicycle. In the clothes of an eighteen-year-old.

The house with the shutters turned into an office building. I no longer know where, in what country to look for it.

Deep within my flesh
a short season
ascends slowly
        slowly
And it's the beginning of another eternity.

(1966)

The Illiterate Man

If you want ...
I tell myself each day: If you want to see the black dogs of your childhood again, give yourself a reason. Throw your hair into the river of lies, plunge, plunge further still into the blood of insanity. Who cares about the masks, but accept it and die if necessary among the bald heads, the slum kids who eat grasshoppers and hot moons, and the black dogs that play in the garbage dumps of the suburbs.
In those days,
the seasons rained colors, the moon rained legendary dragons. The beneficent sky opened onto white horsemen. Just as the coquettish old women sang over the terraces of Casablanca.
One night,
a child lured the moon into a trap.
Ten years later he found it again, old and all pale, even older than the old women without mirrors, the mustachioed grandmothers arguing endlessly like rank rain.
Then,
he understood that the seasons of colors were an invention of the ancestors.
It was
the death of trees, the death of giants. Ghalia bent el Mansour didn't live beyond the seven seas in an emerald castle on the backs of the eagles. He met her in the neighborhood of Ben M'sik or else at the Carrières Centrales, near the fairground kiosks. She wore plastic shoes and prostituted herself with the bicycle repairman.

There was nothing left to do but slam the doors to the sky.
Then, hands ablaze, I restarted the suns.

My illness is a savage world that aims to be without arithmetic or calculations.
I cover the sewers and the garbage dumps.
All the black dogs, all the cockroaches that crawl through my deranged dreams I call friends.
Forgive me and to the devil with you! Love, admire, detest as you see fit.

My factory has no robots, my machines are on strike, the waves of my ocean speak a language that is not yours.
Forgive me and to the devil with you. I am dead and you accuse me of living, I smoke second-rate cigarettes and you accuse me of burning feudal farms.
Listen, listen to me.
According to what law can the chicken fly higher than the eagle?
In its dreams the fish tries to leap to the seventh heaven.
I built terraces and entire cities. Casablanca lived under the American bomb. My aunt trembled in the stairs and thought she saw the sky open by its stomach. My brother M'hammed made Charlot and Dick Tracy dance with the flame of a candle. My mother ...
Must I really go back to the house of the shutters?
The stairs infested with an army of rats, the naked woman with sorceress hands, Allal raping Milouda in a pool of blood, and the Senegalese man cutting off his penis at a butcher's in Derb Al Kabir ...
Must I really go back to the house of the shutters?
The sentinel washes his feet with your tears. Your dearest dream topples over in the savage world of daylight and moon.

You do not stand up.
Your equations in your pockets,
the world on the horns of the ox,
the fish in the cloud,
the cloud in the drop of water,
and the drop of water containing infinity.
The walls of the sky bleed from every pore.
The dogs burst into a savage song. A Kabylian song or a Targuie
legend, perhaps it's simply a tale, and this tale ends by falling into
the stream.
He puts on paper sandals,
goes out into the street,
looks at his feet
      and finds
           that he's walking
                barefoot.
The walls of the sky bleed from every pore.
The wind, the clouds, the land and the forest, the men turned into
traditional songs ...
Behind the sun,
the officers
dig
the tombs.
A man is dead, a 7.65mm bullet to the neck. And there is an old
woman whining, there is another recounting stories of milk and
honey, one about the son of a nasty lumberjack who wins half a
kingdom by decapitating a ghoul's seven heads ...
The thrilled wind suddenly rises to its knees,
extinguishes the fire under the pot,
tumbles down the stairs and
goes to play on the cobblestones of rue de Monastir telling the same

lewd stories to the surrounding windows. My chest full, my eyes
on fire, the houses and the terraces and even the sun, emerged from
an empty silo, break through the ceiling all the way to my bed.
My hair

     or my hands

         rediscover

            the use of speech.

For the things I loved the most
I want to keep my memory intact ...
The places—the names—the actions—our voices.
A song is born. Was it a song?
For the things I loved the most
I want to keep my memory intact. But, suddenly,
it happens:
Places get confused with other places, names slip one by one to
their deaths.
A blue hill spoke. Where was it?
A song is born. My memory wakes up, my steps no longer know
the paths, my eyes no longer know the house or the terraces, the
house in former days filled with flowers and a rosary from the
Kaaba. The world, no bigger than a newspaper. In this world,
there is no delirious wind or dancing houses
behind the sun

     there are

        officers

            digging

                tombs

and
in the silence
the roar of shovels
replaces the song.

Victor Hugo drank from a skull to the health of the barricades. Mayakovsky disrupted the clouds in the radio cities. We had to search for the flute of vertebrae in the cemeteries of the future. Today, I must defuse the love songs, the butterflies smoke pipes, the flowers have wolf's skin, the innocent birds get drunk on beer, some even hide a revolver or a knife. My heart rented a bachelor pad between my legs.
Let's go,
wake up, men.
Will the children of the sun still end up as
sweepers and beggars?
Where did he go, the man that made the dead in the countryside tremble? and the man who, bending his arm, shattered a sugar-loaf? and the man who disappeared by the entrance to the sewers after overturning a battalion of trucks and jeeps?
All the memories are open,
but the wind has swept away the words,
but the streams have swept away the words.
We are left with
        strange words
a strange alphabet
            that would be astonished to see a camel.

The bard went quiet.
To take shelter from the rain, Mririda threw herself into the stream.
At school, we eat oats.
The secret password no longer sets you free.
Will that child never recover? My sister, prepare him the recipe I mentioned, and don't forget to crush the bird in the mortar, it's good for the health! But really, what does he suffer from?
You see, my father wasn't in the war. He inherited from his ancestors

a trunk full of books and manuscripts. He spent entire nights reading them. Once, he fell asleep, and when he woke up, he went crazy. For fifteen days, he believed he was living in a very, very deep well. He furiously dug and dug, but never managed to reach groundwater. He was extremely thirsty. On the sixteenth day, my mother made a precious talisman for him that restored his reason. Except, that day, he became illiterate. He didn't even know how to write his name. When he found the trunk again, he took an ax and smashed it to pieces. My mother used the wood to cook the head of the sheep for Eid al-Adha, the Sacrifice Feast.

To this day, when I ask my father what happened to the books and the manuscripts, he looks at me for a long time and says:

I believe, I do believe that I left them at the bottom of the well.

(1967)

Memory Fourteen

Happy is he whose memory rests in peace.
Whether the earth bears or does not bear,
whether the streams flow with honey or blood,
whether our gaze is blinded or cut off,
our memory endures—
may it regain the rhythm of our twenties.

I remember the morning of maledictions,
the city streets beaten to death,
the sun among the empty books,
and the houses from my bicycle, I remember.
Now history
shatters in the vertigo of blood:
a tale arises with each step.
Like a sordid vine the song
sets its foot on my chest ...
the leprous horsemen ...
the snake asleep in a woman's warmth ...
the snake transformed into a silk belt ...
The thousand-year-old miracle, I remember.
Now,
now the forest advances,
now the trees, to each its own name, its civil status
its genealogy,
now the mountains, now the springs,
the rivers, the oceans, now the deserts
stop at the bottom of the ramparts.
No more

song,
no more
history,
no more
apathy.
The ancestors on the luggage racks,
the ancestors light-years away from my words.
Now the wind and its companion, the tambourine.
What about the wind and the tambourine?
Now the sixty verses, 300,000 knives
planted in flesh and blood.

Now,
Now the 14 generation
learning curses.

At the beginning,
there were
tombs all day long.
The maniacal wisdom of the Sacred Books.
As for men,
as for beasts,
they were born armored with mud and sickness.
The plow composed songs,
the millstone composed songs,
the marmite filled with bombast ...
He came,
the mute prophet
who had no childhood.
I remember the hair scrubbed
with hyena shit,

and the angels assassinated in the latrines ...
I remember the dismembered sky,
the galaxies with their warm guts,
and the stray cats
who were kicked
in the temples
by our heels.
I remember the telephone wires, the madwomen of Casablanca,
   the child fed by the earth, by seasons and spit—they bought
   him alchemical babouches, they taught him about the prophet
   ancestors, the fkih-barber-dentist-genealogist circumcised him
   at the foot of the vase, and the old woman, the little shriveled
   up old woman told him: Don't dig wells when you have a
   spring! What tree hasn't been rattled by the wind? If you want
   honey, plunge your hands into the apiary! ...
And I learned the fables by the feet of verse.
I made a pillow out of the sun.
The sky on its knees on my bed: a kite universe.
My blood,
my blood inhabited by horses, I remember.
Who will ransack that fake legend
of the young girls who lost their hair in the magic fountains?
Who will ransack the legendary mornings
when the sky opened
by its stomach
onto white horsemen?

Years of the gazelle,
years of the locusts,
year of the sword and the canon,
year of the fair season.

Our blood still tastes like legend.

Who will learn the illiterate songs, the thorns in the soles of the
    feet, a caravan of rundown people hunted by the plague and
    trachoma, Bni Kalboun to the east, Bni Ara to the west ...
    Aye!

Aye little mother,

tell me about the silos of Doukkala,

tell me about Jebel Akhdar,

sing me Hayna's lament ... Hayna, Hayna, what will you eat for
    dinner, where will you sleep tonight? My dinner is oats and
    my bed among the dogs!

Aye little mother,

in this country of twilights,

we suffer seven times a death that never ends.

The blind name the meteors,

the legless jump the walls,

the giants into the cow's ear,

the mules feed on doughnuts.

At the call of the jackals the hills

reply, Present,

and the blessed fleas of God, generations of fleas ...

Ouak ouak!

What is this crowd in rags, chanting the lunar miracles at two in
    the morning? What is this horde of beggars in the prehistoric
    labyrinths of Massa? Will the Mahdi return on the back of a
    donkey in the middle of the twentieth century?

Where are you,

you, the poet that lost your tablets at Ouijjane,

you who were walking barefoot, your stomach empty,

out to conquer the solar system?

What poet?

What poet, reaching the edge of the world, will hang the little
  leather bag containing his journey's provisions on a star?
I saw
the sky filled with lead, I saw the cities reduced to silence, I saw
  death in its thick cotton pants, it was welcome everywhere,
  it took the petit taxis or else it went on bicycle, sometimes it
  even jumped on the telephone wires, on the shutters and the
  terraces, and straddled the clouds above the slums.
Nothing left
but the excremental wisdom,
of such old jackals,
tamed,
surprised in their sky of fear and locusts.

Here,
we burned all the forests,
we drank the last drop.
Eyes no longer suffice.
All the insane words, the half-clothed songs, the songs struck with
  cold bodies, the halka at the bottom of a well ... My friend
  the tambourine is dead, we threw its cadaver to the hyenas.
Here I stop.
Here I am among no one.
Only the madmen hear the clamors.
The savage brain,
a cemetery of laughs and sarcasm.
At the bottom, all the way at the bottom of my arteries,
my song gallops
across the supine bodies.
I am standing among the fresh tombs.

(1969)

Remember Sinbad

someone
remembers
Sinbad
and
plunging
their hands into the water
believes they seize
a living
cloud.

What to Say

I think of the sordid streets of Casablanca
of the silent mornings
odors of Brazilian coffee
odors of rancid god
odors of bleeding dreams
I think of the too-recent day of death
and of madness
I think of those who go
far away to live out the end of a glacial tale
I think of those who stay
or who cannot go far away
or who are shut in, cut off from the sundial.

Soon I'll know what to say.

Give Me Back My Storms

So, one Friday, I decided to fly away from the house with the shutters. Not like a swallow, as sooner or later swallows return to the telephone wires, but like a cloud, one of those black December clouds, elusive horse made of wind and fresh wool, recklessly stomping minarets and terraces, and sometimes even the crowds.

I was not a cloud made of wind or wool, carried far to the south, having lost my shoes and shirt above Casablanca. I believe it was Grandmother Yamna's fault. Unless.

No. It was definitely Grandmother Yamna's breath that carried me away.

Oh, it wasn't her intention to send me so far: a little stroll along a field of poppies on the border of the city. Except the wind that Friday of December wasn't in the mood to go easy on flimsy bodies. Rapidly I became a black dot in the sky.

So, that Friday, without permission, a rebel armed with the future (it's dangerous, the future!), I took off with the speed of a galloping horse, drunk on stars, unbridled. No time to say goodbye to my childhood friends. I imagine them still there, intact, dreaming of morning bicycle rides and chocolate bars. Sometimes I see them in bands, barefoot or with their too-big shoes, jumping on carts, imitating the Sioux in heat beneath the window of the little Algerian woman ...

I flew over other cities
other villages where other bands

were playing with their childhoods
and I actually cried

But I didn't cry over the morning odors or the twilight games when
the woman revealed herself to our feverish eyes

I didn't cry over the filmmaker's madness
Tarzan lost in the Bahia in a jungle of enormous rats
plaguing the cresyl and the old garments.

I didn't cry over the seven hills or the poppy field where the ogre
was shouting to the clouds: "Give me back my thunder! Give me
back my storms!" Or the nights of Ramadan when the whole city
would play the lottery while, between the stars, amidst widespread
indifference, the Messenger of light passed by …

No, really, I didn't cry over all those things.

Like the man who crossed the Tarfaya desert
all the way to the submerged cities to witness the sacrifice of the
camel,
I returned to a city of bleeding sidewalks
Someone cried at the top of their lungs: "Get rid of the cadavers!"
Scarcely had we made the first one disappear when a second one
sprang up, more terrible than the first.

No, really, I didn't cry
I was very young then
Didn't they always used to say to me: "You are too young Sidi
Ahmed!" or else: "You have your whole life ahead of you!"
The time ahead of me lived in the melodies of old gramophones.

Our mornings were cold.
In front of the doorway to the Mohammadia School, the newspa-
per spread before our eyes, we deciphered death
and death, unbeknownst to us,
our death
occurred several times ...

Children
when you are carried away in the wind unexpectedly
it is rare to find the way back again.
The door to childhood is barely,
barely visible at the horizon
it closes as soon as you have crossed the threshold.

May Childhood and All Childhoods

May childhood and all childhoods rot in the American depot and
may the swallow-children be spared from mourning them.
There is no more blood on the sidewalk
Look
On this sinister night of December 1976, the barefoot stories
shiver between our walls in our sick chests
Look, isn't that Scheherazade—Scheherazade-the-Morning—that
old woman with no memory with no genitals, that old toothless
woman unable to blow out a candle?
For ... for thirty years already each year at the same hour in the
rain in the mud the vomit or the rust she arrives limping covered
in the latest rags to knock on our doors
Do you hear her?
Do you hear her over your televisions?
She leaves
head lowered
on golden roads
Someone stops her to say hello
mistaking her for merciful death
she does not respond and
when she is sure that no one can see her
she jumps on a white horse and returns
to deserted Baghdad

May childhood and all childhoods rot in the American depot and
may the swallow-children be spared from mourning them
There is no more blood on the sidewalk

Look
On this sinister night of December 1976 ...
Why don't you say it?
Are you afraid you'll be buried alive in the silo?
Are you afraid you'll be draped in the leper's coat as Prince Égaré
was in the past?
Or that your mouth will be filled with dirt and maggots?
or that your head will be hung by the hair from the crenels of
feudal times?

My generation
cursed generation born of the marriage of the louse and the locust
dreaming of colonial brothers dreaming of rape and blood and
mountainous genitals

Monsieur, I was born during World War II but it was not my birth
that caused the cataclysm, I swear. Without asking me they cir-
cumcised me, they baptized me Mohamed like my father and my
grandfather, then they said to me: Happy are the slumdogs who
fear God! I raised my eyes to the sky and saw Allah armed with
a bludgeon transplanted from Heaven. Since I fear God, I do not
have any money to marry but I practice daily at the brothel. Glory
to the French colonials!

Monsieur, I was born in 1941. To send me to school my father,
clever man, pretended I was two years younger. Since then, I
haven't stopped running to catch my real birthday!

Monsieur, I don't know when I was born. When he fornicates, my
father doesn't typically stop himself to write down the date!

For me, Monsieur, I believe he did stop. That's probably why my mother died during childbirth. I showed up on a Thursday morning at eight o'clock sharp July 1939 and a lot of good it does me to know that, seeing as no degree, no work!

I studied all my life for my degrees and I stopped only when there wasn't any more space in my head to store even one more comma! Work? Apparently we'll have to wait for the resurrection of the Mahdi!

Monsieur, I can't stop getting hard. Since childhood I've dreamt of European asses and thighs! Except we gained Independence a bit too early and all the blondes took off!

Don't push! I, too, have something to say, it's burning up my intestines and my testicles. But for God's sake I can't remember the words! It's like there's a well at the bottom of my skull.

So just shut up! What I have to say is of the utmost importance! Because I am an inspector, and very soon a commissioner, if you please. They amuse me, the boys who know how to read and write like doctors! What good is that when I'm better?

Pfft! How could a guy like you be valuable in the eyes of a guy like me? Buffoon that I am ...

Monsieur, I betrayed everyone, I don't even know where my mother lives anymore ...

Cursed generation born of the louse and the locust! May childhood and all childhoods rot in the American depot and may the swallow-children be spared from mourning them!

There is too much blood on the sidewalks

And what is it that you do not say,
poet starved for texts
Here you are
a Friday in the month of Rajab
listening to the desert
A story taps at your window
an old story
rainbowish
with heads hands hair
and postcards of Casablanca
And what is it that you do not say
poet starved for texts
Break the window
Spit in the face of angels on airplanes
Trample on the big cloud of Arabia
Here you are
a Friday in the month of Rajab
listening to the desert.

Gold and Blood

In Abyssinia in Ethiopia I can't remember ...
Who sailed night after night,
dreaming of miniature savages, without ever
reaching the last night where the sun
rose from the foot of the bed?
Nothing but luminous battles
in the house with the shutters!
Nothing but mute meetings, nothing but dead people!
Only warriors in metal
bathed in gold and blood
crying under their masks
for childhoods greased with arrows and the Quran!
Childhood, my childhood with its stench of seaweed and trenches!
Childhood, my childhood where
sorcerers' recipes
were handed down
between two death throes!
My childhood
with its maw of bloody religion, my childhood
with its maw of a mother with an injured liver
urinating on morning crepes!
Childhood, my childhood
on a badly traced Congo river ...
Upon waking one had to jump like a goat
on the back of a grandmother, one had to ...
How can you still roam
between uninhabited tales and lands
with your hands in your pockets?

Or populate with ancient warriors
the slums of Ben M'sik and the Carrières Centrales?
Or else spread out naked
penis in a timid cloud
on the edge of a torrent sweeping along our friends' cadavers?

There Are Those

There are those who say
thank you
in the morning air
who are surprised by nothing
not even by the ox carrying the world on its horns

There are those at peace
in the slums
who hear the jets of water of Scheherazade
and who search every night
for the Hesperides' golden apples

There are those who fall into debt
for the entire year of Hegira
and who, the celebration over, end up on the ground
without knowing what they are waiting for

There are those who count the days
and others who already know the hour
They ask nothing
They die just like the morning light

There are those still counting the days
but what days are they counting?

In times past
we erected golden statues
in memory of the poets

In our country
out of Muslim charity
we dig them tombs,
and with their mouths filled
with dirt, our poets
keep on screaming.

To the Poet Prisoners

Misfortune to he who laid a hand
on the poet prisoners
Happy are the poet prisoners
my friends
intact in this kingdom
Inside me each day
I hear the echo of the padlocks
that hold you back
Inside me in my blood
you immense vigilant have succeeded
in penetrating the labyrinths under the ramparts
But
here's one now (no use naming you)
meager disheveled a sky in your eyes
and secret birds
As soon as the guards turn their backs
he flies
he comes to greet us
and often despite the fatigue
he crosses the sea
The birds know you
There are shreds of cloud in your beard
wipe them off before going back to the walls
Happy are my friends
the poet prisoners
for beneath the earth they see
much further than us
No tombstone can contain them.

We Must

We must question the mountain
to find out how
our warriors died

We must ask the ocean
how our men
met their deaths
in the marine prisons

We must ask the wind
where all the words went,
the words spoken
for the heart and for dignity.

How Many

How many stars
does it take to make a man?
How many futures must we imagine,
how many cemeteries,
platoons, silences?
Our stolen
youth
applauds with a single hand.

I would like
one day
to fly up high
rid of
myself.

Some Truths to Say Nothing

1
You say: It's written.
This book is not a cloud.

2
The invention of the loudspeaker
makes the minarets so small.

3
When you are hungry
read the Quran.
Will you be sated?

4
People: Your god is unique?
Your enemy as well.

5
Silence is golden.
I have never seen a mute get rich from it.

6
A child covers himself with god
and wakes up with god.
What a shroud.

7
Do not say: I am hungry.
Say: Who is starving me?
Do not say: He's illiterate.
Have you ever seen a poet's diploma?

Love Poem for Naïma

I would have liked to write nothing but love poems
I too would have liked
to take the morning in my arms
inhale its light its dew
To burst the clouds for fun
steal the Milky Way
leap from petal to petal
possess the strength of nectar and of the breeze
I would have liked for us
to sink our teeth into poetry
the same way we sink our teeth into tales
But the tales no longer taste like fruit
We condemned the ogre and the ogress to death
because they didn't count their beads
among the odors of mats and mosques
we burned alive
the beautiful lover who transformed into springs
I too would have liked to say my love
despite the mud despite the blood
I would have liked to say: I love you
as one might have said: I am alive
I would have liked to say my childhood to forget
the famine of our neighborhoods
to forget the swallows in rags
and to forget the minarets planted in our flesh
I would have liked to conjure a blue sky
soft clouds with a soft poppy skin
I would have liked

to drive the mountain's echoes mad
to the sounds of the tambourine and the hastily carved flute
to teach modern dances
to the bee and the orchard bird
to teach new rhythms even to the cricket ...

My Country

I

My country has lived for centuries off of the lies of the dead.
So it is only natural that we build sanctuaries where we heal our
insane.

II

Look a little behind our sick pupils, you'll find children chained
up inside of stomachs, subjected by force to the seven waves of an
infected mythology, where, if you ask them, horsemen of light will
tell you in tears about the tribal epics of certain ancestors, trapped
like rats in snow and blood.

III

Our arteries gorged with such soft blood.
We water the others' orchards, and the others, turbaned, draped
in the perfumes of wretched Arabia,
writing,
with strokes of swords and merciless verses,
a History
that is never ours.

IV

You see,
first we built in the sand
and the wind carried away the sand.
Then we built in the rock
and the lightning broke the rock.
We should seriously think about building
in men.

V

The farmer observes that the tree is barren.

He examines the soil.

Who among us, with daring or simple innocence, unleashed that vile amalgam of putrid brains marinating in the terrors of apocalypse, of hell and heaven with its entrance fee?

Who among us, listening intently, was not broken in two by the screams of our dead?

It is true that our sky is full of the clamor of buffoons.

It is true that our mornings, our childhoods, are endlessly woven into the threads of a starched East, which wears detachable collars and bow ties, strutting in stolen tangos. That East rushed to bury their poets under metric tons of the Quran.

I said it: Our sky is full of the clamor of buffoons.

Listen to them all day long opening coffins for our impatient dreams.

I hear them, even from afar,
gagging our feeblest dreams.

They proclaim in the microphones: Our Middle Age capitals were lit up with neon while the Christians of the West were groping in the shadows!

And again:

Remember our illustrious men of war!

Remember our illustrious men of science!

I ask you: Must we live and die in recollection like those paralytic grandmothers who can no longer distinguish between a black thread and a white thread?

VII

Today I want to say it: This silence hides death out loud.

Are we the children stuffed with a fourteen-century-long farce?

We swapped our ears for foul-smelling shells listening to an ocean asleep like a tapestry at the bazaar.

VIII

Our memory sick with the future.

Death strolls on the clean sidewalks. It reads the newspaper backward, pupils drowned in cruel stalemates and shooting ranges where the birds lost their voices.

We weren't aware of death's presence, but isn't that what childhood is? May we be pardoned for closing our eyes on the battlefield, we confused bloodstains and poppy stains. A chariot came toward us, flattening our laughs and our marbles. The ogre bore the face of the tenant next door. On winter nights, his wife, the ogress, would prepare traditional couscous made with lice and naughty kids. During the day, she would turn into a scavenger or a leper, hurling insults in French or Spanish, constantly sliding into buses to puke up her catastrophes ...

Our mythology opened onto underprivileged neighborhoods. Our princes reigned over the nearby Atlantises. A cloud or a wink was enough to land in porphyry palaces.

Above the palaces a grandmother's laugh surprised us like a sudden storm.

We found ourselves seated, poor and injured, shivering on a sheepskin around the familial teapot.

IX

Wretched companions of the Grotto!

Here we are caught, at the end of the night, in the trap of the light.

Who we are.

Impoverished, our memory hesitates. It wants to crouch down like a beast of burden in the night oasis.

Crouching memories! Let's dream of the survival of Scheherazade-the-Morning! Let's dream of a Baghdad at the end of the street! Let's prepare to suffer the death of our ancestors covered in Persian ornamentations who, in their silk shrouds, desperately attempt to erase every defeat for a slow eternity.

Five Memories Minus One

The Horsewoman

I had an ordinary dream, the dream of an ancestor
I remember: Beneath a sky of ancient red,
I held the horsewoman by the halter.
Because I trapped the prophetic thoroughbred,

the crowd praised me through the nameless town.
Veiled concubines awaited my presence,
warriors in gold armor and renowned
dignitaries surprised by my adolescence.

Never had a tribe received a more triumphant reception.
A bit of cloud in her wings, the horsewoman
astounded the wise men, and even the children.
She carried a nest of swallows within her bosom.

Barely visible beneath their bulbous turbans,
on the fringes of ever-growing ovations,
the theologians of the empire, sullen
that such an angel could exist in the world without them,

prepared to discover in their missals
that there's a special corner of hell for hybrids
and that this kind of demon, real or unreal ...
We can't escape from ulemas or wrinkles!

I was imprisoned for being a false prophet.
If I hadn't escaped through the ceiling,
they would have immediately split open my head
to strangle the demon living inside me!

Fleas and Vowels

I soon learned that a silk thread was the only divide
between heaven and hell, and that functionaries,
winged, white, unable to laugh or cry,
were inscribing our acts in a great dictionary.

A hunchbacked god prayed between flowers.
On the floor below, a sentinel,
whipping the vanquished, cheered on the victors
who were smiling between fleas and vowels.

On the school's terrace, the warriors
in the golden armor of antiquity's slaughters
buried each day, among the coral,
beneath our sleeping skulls, their living daughters.

When the armed prophet descended into the crowd
and rustled in a beautiful cloud of Arabia,
the hunchbacked god, our fkih, knelt on the ground,
and forgot his market in his mania.

Since then, our joyous mischievous sleep
has wrapped us up in ghastly cyclones
that assassinates our songs silently.
And heaven is now rendered in monotone.

Our poets die of homesickness.
The wind carries them off like dead leaves.
We see them sometimes keeping sad company
in cafés where, to escape their sadness,
they transform into flies, without a peep.

Their legs soak in peaceful storms.
Staring into empty glasses they imagine hell
or heaven while humming an old tune
from the gramophone. When they set forth,
heads lowered, into the red blaze of a torch,
the poem stops short.

The wind carries them off like dead leaves.

Today, death will throw its dirty laundry
on the city. What city? Casablanca.
I'm not making it up, read it, it's in the paper.
It's not there? Oh, well. I read it somewhere.
So, it will rain laundry on your yards,
a mix of fleas and dreams, of blood
and urine, in your spacious boulevards!
Death will hail songs on all your heads!
Who am I? I always forget to introduce myself.
I walked out of an old photograph.
I don't need an ID
to scatter my dirty laundry behind your walls.

                                                        (1977)

Prophecies in Chalk

I

Numb with cold, choking beneath my hair,
here I am, poor, naked, in the bright sun's glow.
Will I recognize my childhood's dishonor?
Will I be able to climb higher than my toes?

From my ancestors I inherited no palace,
no turbaned God or silos or diamonds.
I cannot find in their golden sky
the place where they still fast, that paradise.

Cemeteries vanished in sad legends!
I still see you: the weeping dead with no hands,
like old children frightened of feeling the chagrin
of letting your tomorrows be stolen …

Miserable lineages of prophets!
You wanted to invent emerald palaces
for us, and it's at the bloody fêtes
where mules reign, decorated with gold flourishes!

Leave behind your clichéd heaven,
your Quran clouds, your wind and rain shrouds!
But don't be surprised by our age. Often,
it's our dreams that make us old.

No one will come on this stormy eve.
Your darkened skeletons, chained to the Quran ...
I will rummage, page by page, through eternity,
until the last of my kin are dead and gone!

II

They assassinate my words, they murder my past.
Must I, too, carry the shroud deemed sacred,
the fake cold shroud of your atrocious darkness,
and your kingdoms killed by the devoured verses?

Must I, too, straddle your old dreams?
Forgive me, I cannot. I am of another generation.
I live between furious blood and peace.
And my childhood is long forgotten.

III

My eyes open onto secret seasons.
Now my sky is no longer bloody.
What will we do with that lazy horizon
where they coddle us with useless melodies?
Look at our shelves. The white horsemen sleep
through our sorrowful adolescence.
We don't straddle the slow wind in our dreams!
Tombs await us, full of silence.
Even into death may our dreams journey,
perhaps they will moor in some haven,
a world where prisons are ancient ruins.
Hybrid hope of a languid poem,
deaf to the chants of a mythic generation
like a kite, straddling its history!

IV

The spring will no longer remember its colors.
I imagine it stomping on the skyline.
Who plots the ambush of the years of cinder?
Our seasons hang from the new streetlights.

Never again will the wind evoke legend.
A people without memory is a people without name.
May they dream of the antique splendor of Samarkand!
Kingdoms in rags from whence we came!

The wounded poets without faces will no more
celebrate the songs that steal away time!
Our tombs will take off during sad storms
to search for our joyful springtimes.

Our tombs will search forever.
Strange trees will grow over our heads.
And they will judge us at our age, and our judges
will erase our tombs and our language.

V

I who sank in channels like rain
between hollow tombs and the blossoming dead.
I who formerly cultivated life as I desired
without distinguishing tomorrow from today.
I who guided the clouds through the tempests
like a God born from the specks and spray of sea.
Here I am, begging way at the back of my head,
for some sun in my people's country.

VI

A bird on a branch
dies with our forgotten childhoods
in the villages.
A fragile night
like a child's smile
and the few fits of insanity when we threw away gold.
May a just century restore our seasons
and our sight!
Walls built right in the middle of our flesh ...
Still, I imagine islands erected
in our meager sleep.
Like a deranged cigarette,
our mythology
consumes itself
in an adolescent's dream.

VII

Between me and my secret this cursed
poem forever returns at a furious gallop.
Even if I have to kill what I love in myself,
I will reach the bottom of these dreams
planted with romantic forests.
I can see I must decapitate this magic sky
where my ancestors trample invisible fruits.
But the ramparts prop up the seventh heaven!
But the shutters are still there, perhaps!
In my blood the rivers of milk and honey, on
the edge of these rivers of never-ending dunes, on the edge
of these dunes, the stories in slippers with their
falsely serene eyes, secretly burying bloodied stars ...
Let's go! We must climb the forty-one steps!
Here is the scenery of childhood or desert ... And I
who believed I would find the throng of an ark! Quickly, grant me
a liar's imagination! I see ... yes, I see
the beautiful Scheherazade,
weak light of the house with the shutters!
The shutters open
onto a sad Baghdad ...
Here I am again, shipwrecked
between rats and parents.
Under my bed the acrobats,
the dreams of the forty, surrounded by treasure ...
A public square, and the fair, and the old women of times past
hurling curses at youths in love
with rum, with battlefields without wounds ...
On the sidewalks, the leprous beggars, panting,

and the nameless whores of Casablanca
with deceitful eyes, mincing the songs of Asmahan ...
From between our teeth come powerful legends
and strange poems from Isfahan!
From Isfahan or elsewhere ... I imagine. The cities
melt onto our dreams to devour them.
Our prophecies,
we drew them in chalk ...!

(1977)

Story of Sinbad
By Way of an Epilogue

Prologue

This is not a hotel room.
Not all those who wish to sleep here may.

Perhaps I am a tree.
Oak tree, fig tree, argan tree, I can't remember.
And it's not my fault
if I feel my leaves falling.

I do not swear by the rising wheat,
I do not swear by sweat or blood.
I do not shake your hand.
I need oxygen,
and so I flee from suffocation.

Today we breathe more easily
in a tomb.

But not so fast!
Don't open the tombs!
Their ashes will cover your face
with sky, with flesh, with childhoods, with cruel days.
For if the living often dream the dreams of the dead,
the dead undream the dreams of the living.

1

In a café-bar,
the counter, like a whore, distances itself.
A tale told with the shots of a revolver,
a tale for two for eternity
takes by storm
the skull in the form of a dark blue cloud.

2

The skull rolls
between pitiful warriors
and even more pitiful gastropods.

3

Then,
like a diluvial ark,
the skull drops anchor into a world
of faded roads.

4

That's why the tribes ask themselves:
Where are we going?

5

So the skull, throwing caution to the wind, proclaims itself a
prophet, like the prophet of Khorassan, but without a sword,
without miracles, without a golden mask. It's a skull in the form
of a dark blue cloud, I think I said that already.

6

In a sanctuary (a cadaver ditched at the horizon), crabs devour a white horse, or the white horse devours the crabs. Go find yourselves in those shadows (it's common knowledge that all the caretakers of the sanctuaries sell candles). For the moment, the old woman, surrounded by vultures and votives, plucks the feathers from an angel, a moronic angel disguised as a rooster.

7

In a dream,
police inspectors handcuff you:
In the name of the law, shut your mouth!

8

So you must abandon the dreams.

9

But it's not easy to rid yourself of a dream.
A dream is not a dirty sock.

10

When the jug is empty it must be refilled.

11

The dream
like the filled jug
slakes thirst.
But a dream, when we don't know how to grab hold of it, kills.

12

Having proclaimed itself a prophet,
the skull rolls all the more through the crowd ...

13

"What you're saying is all very nice, but who sent you to unveil
these truths?"
"No one," replies the skull.
"God didn't send you?"
"I confess to not having met anyone in the course of my journey
who fits the description."
"As for the description ..."

14

In the sanctuary,
the saint's legs stretch.
Through the catafalque,
the skull senses a resurrection
in seven tiers.
A matter of weight and size.

15

A grocer consults our books. A grocer without an age, without
a family name, an infected enigma that our generations drag
through their sick arteries when they can't easily uncover it in
a pillow. Whoever says pillow says trap. And so consultation,
judgment, stampede. Have some manners, what the hell! Go,
bands of resurrected, at the first sight of these skeletons! Mes-
sieurs the ambassadors, duly noted! You, wrinkly guy, get in line
like everyone else! His lordship refuses the shroud? His lordship
prefers a gold pinafore perhaps? ...

16

The feathers of the angel
disguised as a rooster fly away.
A blessing for the naked angel.

But the naked angel swims a bit farther away.

17

Let's describe the naked angel.

> Don't wander off just yet, angel.
> There will still be time to leave like a package at the
> post office with the label FRAGILE on your back.

A naked angel is a vine leaf on a donkey's genitals. It's also the
name of all the domesticated statues playing hopscotch with one
leg on the bloody sidewalks. In the turbaned poems, he shines
with a magnesium light, sings with the voice of the swan or the
lover, a scarecrow lover, draped in religion, dreaming of America
in the pupils of the beloved.

18

The naked angel then swims a bit farther away.
Scenery of Egypt and Asia. Royal attics at the end of a sleepwalk-
ing spotlight. Maximum effect. The rainbow collapses abruptly,
outside the cardboard theater devised by a fortune teller. The
fortune teller didn't have to work too hard. All she had to do
was strip the clichéd images of a Babylon flat as a hand.

19

Behind the angel a large matron
(seven breasts—seven heads—seven vaginas).
A bunch of keys on her belt.

But it is forbidden to touch the keys.
In dreams, it is always forbidden to touch the keys. Consult the dictionary of prohibitions. Your pockets will be stuffed with useless treasures. Your castrated horses will fly no higher than a gob of spit. And in your garden perfumed with musk and sperm, you risk circumcision at the end of each page ...! No. No free consultation. Let me tell you about the rest of the scenery. You will decide later.

20
In front of the angel, seven waves ready, mouth open.
Beyond the seven waves, artificial satellites with ice cream in the wings.
Beyond the artificial satellites, the skull grappling with police inspectors.
"As for the description ...!"
A brave man passes him the handcuffs.
This isn't a life anymore, says the skull. We aren't even safe in our dreams!

21
Finally,
the naked angel swims.
The maternal sea
seizes it suddenly by the neck.
Welcome to the land of carnivores!

22
Curtain.

23

Don't applaud. Stay seated.
Count your flies and your lice again,
belch your propitiatory slogans,
arm yourselves with a pickaxe and a shovel and win the bet.
Nothing will save you from reptiles.
Maggots don't pay rent!

So,
open the tombs!
The dead await you!
They will drape you in a custom-made shroud.
They will tell you of the horrendous Thousand and One Nights!
And Scheherazade-the-Morning
will impersonate for you, and only you,
the cry of the dead-of-love,
the cry of the dead-of-hunger,
the cry of the dead-of-sex,
the cry of the dead-of-plague, the dead-of-thirst, the dead-of-
    Quran or Gospel, the dead-of-solitude, the dead-of-sadness,
    the dead-of-torture, the dead that keep dying the dead in the
    newspapers who wriggle through their ametropic nightmares
    the dead of vomit of words empty of rain the dead at eighteen
    the.

(1976–1977)

PHOTOGRAMS

Les mots, les mots
Ne se laissent pas faire
Comme des catafalques.

Et toute langue
est étrangère.

Words, words
Resist
Like catafalques.

And every language
is foreign.

—GUILLEVIC, "ART POÉTIQUE"

Our country has no more warriors
only timeworn fig trees beaten thoroughly by
the thousand winds of misfortune.
The barefooted angels with pathetic faces
die with each new dawn
at the bottom of our bastions.
The scent of childhood is now nowhere to be found
no nursery rhymes or sunshowers.
What happened to the ancient romance, our dreamy
obsession with the horsewoman's powers?
Oh, that horsewoman with the mane longer
than the clouds over our houses crumbling
on and on
beneath our meager adventures!
Now what days will open
onto our prisons plastered with stars
and 100 miles of silence?

I see a horizon cracked in two
Our youth refuse to be born there a second time
Their hatred of the past has no equal
except for their repeated failed suicide
in the margins of newspaper articles
At each celebration
they draw wrinkles on themselves
Their happiness sports carnival masks
My blue sky between two eclipses of swallows tells of war all the
    tall volcanoes of long ago. In the lava recklessly we forged
    fantastic lives in which we were kings
This sky today
looks like a postcard
Does it remember
the locusts of Sudan?
They are dead
dead dead our stars leave a trace
of toothache or straw fire
in the blood of September

But it's no longer permitted for lovers
in the cinema to uncover each other.
Would I also be among this herd of birds
in May plunging headfirst into electric poles
for no apparent reason?
Our loves in black and white
snuffed out each day resuscitated by way of
old splenetic songs
we would recite in class or in the courtyard ...
During winter we would play
hide and seek every night with death
in the unbearable cold of our little streets
we were crazy about the pretty European girls
and an America of vibrant luminosity
emerged from the utopia of a certain Cecil B. DeMille
to whom we forked over our fortunes wholeheartedly ...

I want to translate the blood
that still lies in the realm of childhood
and the thousand cracked seasons stacked with the flesh of
pale dawns and images in which we endlessly shatter ourselves
And cross the threshold of memory of the shutters
one time
one last time
in order to keep intact the inhuman eternity
when we were those little poorly dressed kings
or cruel cowboys and the Comanche without mustangs
escaped from a free film
and unchain along our white lanes
along our famed legends
deprived of impossible fruits
the dark storms of androgynous princesses
with hands of faded satin
and drown in the seven oceans
our distress of a damned galaxy
that no longer knows how to dream ...

I want to translate the last poem's blood
with Casablanca's pinkish blueness
with those old photographs that I love
the battles we fought seemingly endless

And eradicate the wrinkles on all the faces

And repopulate the rainbows with our laughter

And liberate our children from this middle age
our nursery rhymes too
formerly honey-colored

But I have no more words
and my vocabulary has barely
oh barely remained in my two hands

Will we one day be able to
name the fruits of the earth

live in our homes with a human face?

and I compose the poem
a silence broken like a dog's
tooth drips in baroque
words dressed in the blood of hyenas
the night traces dead
leaves on our walls
and on our walls shivers
a skeletal dream
that harbors
all the dead of our Atlantic sea

A Prisoner in Paradise

My grandfather who was young in 1901
had been fighting atop an old horse since dawn

How did he set out to conquer the wind?
He mounted a white cloud, according to him

Can you believe his turban stretched taller than a willow
His saber or his penis at the service of the widow

Sometimes in a dream I see him with my own eyes
He tells me it's truly sad being a prisoner in paradise

Sometimes in the house with the louvered shutters
he appears suddenly with his pockets cluttered

full of maggots. Because he brought us guidance
as he passed through we'd wash the floor in silence

In a sick stench of dead meat he gave a report
of the sky and the heavenly cohorts

in the event of a belated resurrection
And before taking off in no precise direction

the old man honored me with an ashy kiss
Today God no longer permits scandals

and that's why each Friday he escapes from the sky,
my grandfather would often be disguised as a butterfly

or a ladybug, it's true it really happened that way,
unless he simply turned into a ray

of sun skimming the cups of tea
extremely jealous of electricity

He even sat on the tip of my nose
to speak to me of times I was too young to know

of Christians of pretenders and the military
One day he lost himself in the dictionary

there he left behind his babouches and his caban
his amber rosary beads his soul and his turban

Then he ascended into the sky to pay for
having cast a glance at my papers

1948

For a long time
I witnessed God's stomach delight in our dreams
and our dreams would walk barefoot
with rags for heads
among the charlatans and the gnome prophets

At that time
I was the size of a stalk of nettle
The legless elderly
covered in medals
would talk in the streets of times long ago
when they claim sultans governed wearing tattered clothes

Of inexhaustible streams flowing in our pockets

Of thieves in the night
purses heavy, rocketing across the sky
on tiptoe, God observing the angels
Whom can you trust?

The old world had lost its ballads
dressed up in its blood-red garments

Our grandmothers babbled in the toilets
suddenly believing they were back in adolescence

And carrying sad paradises on their backs
and superb clouds white with water and flesh

The ancestors took up the baton of banishment
in a world deprived of its citizenship

Unaware of writing, flies buzzing around our perimeter,
we learned about invisible literatures

We received incredible talismans
crafted by the sorcery of old women

At that time the princess of insomniacs
Surrounded us with strange places and maps

Where a drop of water contained the whole galaxy
And all at once an ant emptied the sea

Our incertitudes were not measured
on the Roman scales. The house of the louvered

shutters closed itself off from all bad things
On the stairs, the angels licked their wings

Others on the terraces covered in dirt
kept watch all day long over their herd

At our doors giants in glasses sang melodies
giants that we mistook at night for dead leaves

With our hands full of wood and incense
we shivered with cold in the warmest nests

On the pavement the wind scattered our dreams
Each day we lost a bit more of our memory

Generation

In 1938 on the night I was born
this country had no more ancestors or History
It was a garbage dump where soldiers on the run
waded in grime and worshipped a deity

who, deaf-mute, twirled in the clouds
among locusts and naked angels
and drunk females done up with storms
Our houses quivered like a hanged morning

and in our alleyways of always meager dinner
the sun shamelessly kissed the spring
The cheeky children left with steps full of cheer
howling about the hunger of soldiers

I grew up unknowingly like a crazy weed
in the bed of venereal nights of Baghdad
I gathered new roles insatiably
and bit the butt of Scheherazade

I rolled my *r*'s with Negritude pride
starving for cirrus clouds and aeroliths
Casablanca tousles through my spine
and in my blood papyrus ink drips

My shipwrecks like audacious blasphemies
drew tender words from love potions
and their teeth tore at the supreme toes of
infamous paradises where one dies elated

Our parties were splattered with urine and blood
Fathers suddenly suffered amnesia and drank
clandestine alcohol with the whole neighborhood
they damned us to the hell of the badly raised

Beware the insolent man who oversteps the cage
of his neighborhood. We would sodomize birds
we would sharpen our rapiers with rage
we indulged in the forbidden we were undeterred

Rachitic knights of the coffee tables
entrenched in our impasses we kept vigil
until bugles pierced the twilights
Sails and invisible paddles

carried us to the redskins the virgin and mysterious
princesses of El Dorado
and the cowboys salved with gold their souls in distress
bleeding like the hogs of Colorado

And in the morning we rediscovered immaturity
and wisdom ambered like archangel buffoons
chanting the Quran in the cemeteries
over all the rag-covered tombs

In that age our meteors shot across
a sky where peaceful God whispered
The bluish windows reflected our frocks
among the stockings and the blonde hair

and our dreams of poets and thieving maggots
became intoxicated with the horsewoman's fragrance
when this old man fresh as a shroud in glasses
welcomed us in the early morning to his rickety palace

where mischievous flies flew us around
The Queen of Sheba all of a sudden
had a vermillion heart in the form of a crown
adorned with dew with crystal and with sun

Beyond our pre-Islamic fortifications
sad heroes and the defeated penniless
faces scarred by ancient afflictions
don't know how to mourn their now-peaceful villages

Sirens steamers and polychrome ensigns
double-locked their horizons imbued
with lemongrass and columbine where men of former times
lived on cruel courage and virtues

Like dogs wearing hatched hope on their sleeves
their tamed cadavers scattered throughout our country
cold planets bigger than our earth and its seas
and beloved tales never on their knees

We braided them like glorious bouquets
or like the quicksilver of our summer nights
All my golden tears accumulated
and my eyes saw the gardens reflected inside

My father breathed in I don't know what space
he dressed himself in blossoms and moons
and lived like a voyager embraced
Upon his brutal death our house died too

My withered mother we called her Madame
In her gaze the firmaments were extinguished
The streets in pants forbidden to women
are the only ones open to welcome her anguish

In her tears float dead stars
swirling in the dawn of a god
with diamond wings slamming like doors
over landscapes of monochrome facades

My older brother lost his childhood in a flash
Horrible hurt sparrows fell from his hands
he closed himself like a page of a love story
that he forgets to read today as he did in the past

Crepuscular photographs in panic
of our stabbing-suckled city
we did not triumph in the Punic Wars
we were too busy playing the lottery

Faubourgs gorged with old Egyptian princes
riding on their bikes through golden republics
speckled with lice from stupid hyenas
they spit laughs in the faces of our perished

And our dead dreaming of a storm of bullets
in the darkness of their mud coffins
fashioned in haste they clung to the ancestors' javelins
(the poor crucified in unseen paintings
bordered with cedar semicolons they strut
immobile in paradise)
We died they said
for a nice big handful
of Indochinese rice but you parasites
what have you—immersed in our shameless murders—
told your poets?
We love France and German beer
like good survivors and the widows
frail as barrels gorged with clouds and moons
but you descendants by accident born during the passing of a
train or a boat and in the bang of a gun that we
leave by an alarm clock and shoes reeking
of fatigue and other people's wars . . .

May our dead no longer speak to us
Our language now kneaded into other woes
with rancid stars a meager pittance
and false kingdoms rich in violent blows

A warring childhood eyes wide open
languishes in a book of ambitious designs
oblivious to a poem of venial devotions
in which the horsewoman perfumed the false skies
In an afterword between the old women
the acrid incense of sweet death in Baghdad
and oppressive kings in atrocious marvels
amaranth Scheherazade flutters about
And us others the jackals of the Numidian deserts
infantrymen of the Protectorate depot
and the flat paradises where humid gazes
give birth to hells and angels that will never be ours
… Our sky is no longer as blue as in childhood
We have riddled with saliva our orphan dreams
and our theological horizon
swallowed like a vulgar mushroom
We have lost all our prehistoric secrets

Time smooths our volcanoes and our eyelids

The house is a blatant imposture of red bricks kneaded with herbs and honey

On its white terrace our sweet injuries wear incredible rainbows around their necks like jewelry

In his wooden bed sleep future cities traced by a child in Chinese ink

There magician friends treat our burns when our adventures dressed in black and white die of desire behind the shutters ...

Fête

In an angel's bed in a wool dress she sleeps
The house is cold the walls white like a dream
motionless death takes a seat
and for two weeks awaits the end of the temporary peace
to count its cadavers devoured by the moon

In an angel's bed in a wool dress she sleeps
In the blast from outside the blood of the fête
repeats the violent myth with gold embroidery
to the snickers of birds and a prophet
who suddenly appeared between bloody books and dunes

In an angel's bed in a wool dress she sleeps
and in her ancestral dream old lunatics
run along the skies bleeding from their whole bodies
toward a silver tower where a thousand firmaments
sip greedily from pale paradises

The paradises were flailing wildly in the halls
there were trees and fruits now archaic
and even archangels pale as a fall night
have come from the distant Adriatic
to be at the fête this Monday night

II

They are the pale archangels treading quietly
I see them floating and our silence breaks
Their poor hearts glazed against our reality
they celebrate as if it were a birthday

The frightened flies leave the bedroom fast
the specters melt into the bed linen
their lunular coats are merely ash
and ash will not erase oblivion

III

The children do not understand that one must stop talking
on the eve of the fête and for a long time they sang
songs that I didn't know when I was young
The aged men count stinkbugs in their coffins

that thrive at the same time as the jujubes
The horizon bears our cavalrymen in one piece
and they dream. With our gunflint weaponry
the centurions will not cross the stream

IV

This Monday of silver- and clay-caused strife
death patiently closes each of its caskets
of ferocious paradises of immobile skies
Before daybreak death will return to the doorstep

The house is cold the savage hills stay mute
bandage the warriors of long ago
My memory is now merely a train station waiting room
where kingdoms without kings sleep forevermore

I have no more shadow I am hardly anything but a shipwreck
that is barely barely echoed by my stare
Grandmother is already on the way to her village
She has imprisoned death in a mirror

Dreams of the Horse

The houses in my country today
escape by playing hooky
to make nice slums in the sky
at the bottom of murals of paradise
with hollyhocks and lilies

They take the sun by its behind
like a kite or a vulgar orange
destroyed by a devastating wind
the wreaths their fingers quickly forge
will be hung in the silence of the concerts

And the young girls become women
overnight and overtake the soldiers at war
In imitation of frolicking children
memory hatches from ancient lore

Bodies with clandestine eyes
swim in ancillary scum
in the middle of fantastic feasts
Now transformed into joyous sanctums

let's scale the dreams of the stallion
in which the ant the dog and the gazelle
join the jackal's gray population
to trace the path of the she-camel

1400

Go go drift
to the rhythm of cheap mythologies
and fearful resurrections with
shrouds and carpets of fleas

Our god is a mammal
illiterate with bloody hands
Hatred of sleepy worlds
smashing camphor and incense

We live in a century of cinders
that pokes its paladins
You cannot buy our future
in the court of worldly harlequins

I leave a long dream brimming with helium
to take a seat like an orphan myth
or like an archangel struck with delirium
in a day filled with marine freshness

and I search for a rhyme rich for my opium
that I will carve in the bathroom on the walls therein
In vain the insane rats have devoured the photo album
of my childhood, a brothel of mescaline

Here I am a pilgrim at the gates of the sun
smashing my galaxies and my soft star
shielded by fake jewels at the bottom of my coffin
where the famished forebears without sails steer
I created a purgatory with no equivalent
that in all seasons my childhood lights up with stars

You must make your dream as you make your bed
My resurrected hell calls for weapons
My blanched childhood turned pale
from memories of suburbs and their racket
My delinquent palace of lapis lazuli
knows all the alarms and all the shipwrecks
Up to the purple horizons of distant Mali
I will recount death with no lies no hysterics
of children born in a tattered silence
where the flea and the louse are waging war
in the middle of sun-drenched cemeteries
and I will tell again of our mischievous ardor
at the bottom of an impasse of an unbuttoned eyelid
before flying away like straw through the wind

My coffin awaits me somewhere at the horizon
I want it to be made of sandalwood and dreams
pinned down like butterflies at the oration
of an adolescence of a brief eternity
May my skeleton blossom with the seasons
may my blood flow freely euphoric
up to the very heart of your solid houses
to the shelter of love to devour your Eves
wreathed in incurable religions
I will be the old earth of Babylon
with its gods its satyrs and its legions
I will spread in your beds my sallow cyclones
and far very far in your shivering regions
I will paint my death on a canvas of autumn

It's an old kingdom of shipwreck
that can no longer laugh nor dream
Does it remember the wildflower
the poets can no longer see?

Its minarets like a scar
its ageless soldiers dead on their feet
and our cries only murmurs
since our god reigns on his knees

With sky and too much silence words like a stubble burning we
choose for ourselves a different childhood

It's an antique kingdom of slow death Draped in days we sleep full
of the empty Full Indeed?

I am condemned to survive
in the thick of a deep swamp
where dismally drunk flowers strive
for a middle age of triumph

My heart sways on the dead branches of trees
to a song so cruel and so melancholic ...

Far from you may my thoughts carry me
toward the city where my future exists

I smooth the unseen new moons
a merry-go-round where I wander ceaselessly

I hate the hypocritical paradises you spew
your angels have killed our memory

The house of recollection has left with the wind
Dead memory will dress me up in cinders
and tamed nights as sad as a convent
nurture the empty smile of salamanders
My ancestors in a shirt of extinguished fire
have grown tired of opening the doors to our dreams
and our dreams locked up in far away
cemeteries of a too-brief eternity
rip open their chests down to their bloody essence
We will have to burn mountains of incense
to erase the sky at the root of our rage
and with our lips sealed with mirages of former days
we will spit as we please with a wounded gaze
on the thousand shutters of a bygone age

Final Photograms

This city escaped from a dream so slow
its light like a tear that remains on the face
of a man who died a thousand years ago ...
Its silver hourglass empties straightaway

Its sad manuscripts its tattered streets
of an age that can no longer recover from absence
its silence is a horizon riddled with the screams
of religion and unhappy adolescence

May a golden cloud disguise itself as a minaret
may rachitic horses dream of fresh pastures
and may a savage poetry be born
between teeth and random colors
I will turn garnet-red death into a masterpiece
more perfect than even a shell's music

A dead book in a plural babble
the sky plucked from 1401
spits horizons of horses without saddles
on the heads of warriors who dream of fortune
like the astrologists obsessed with the million planets
A fragile century burning grass on its knees
unlearns the resurrection of its poets
and the death of an eternity plastered with fleas
Mute memory gives no testament!

And they are reborn from the entrails of the earth
fatigue and the cruel sun render them blind
they no longer have the courage to look backward
they no longer have an age, orphans of world and sky

Above the olive trees the sky is tainted
like their dreams masked in eternal winters
the salt heavier than the embers of hatred
extends the labyrinths in reverse

where they bury their miserable memories
decapitated by silence and wind

and they are reborn like an absence of glory

From the distant villages we hear them often
they are the angels condemned to sadness
all day enveloped in death's loving caress

The light scorns the stone sculptor and saves
a withered minaret from demise
On squalid knees like the five prayers
this Monday's colors have completely lost their cry
I watch the white statues without eyelids
basking in a psychiatric cemetery's moonlight

Beauty born by a stroke of chance
from the whims of fire of sure hands
to be delivered to the lizards
Sad ending to a sweet adventure

It's a hell of backlit changing sky
and a false resurrection colored with
saffron where men live without purpose

In the distance a wrinkle-wounded countryside
hopelessly heats up its little cottages
settled at random among the white stones
It's a postcard of bleeding windows

It lingers even when my eyelids close

Postscript

God of clouds and Books,
your deluge is nothing but
a tear for our drunk hearts
where we gulp down our disgust.

Our blue days: a long succession
of to be continued to be tossed
in the garbage of fleeing generations.

Who will pity us for having lost
the sun that emanates
like an ass of black eternity
and dreams in several volumes
in which the truth fornicates?

New Directions Paperbooks—a partial listing

Javier Marías, Your Face Tomorrow (3 volumes)
Harry Mathews, The Solitary Twin
Bernadette Mayer, Works & Days
Carson McCullers, The Member of the Wedding
Thomas Merton, New Seeds of Contemplation
  The Way of Chuang Tzu
Henri Michaux, A Barbarian in Asia
Dunya Mikhail, The Beekeeper
Henry Miller, The Colossus of Maroussi
  Big Sur & The Oranges of Hieronymus Bosch
Yukio Mishima, Confessions of a Mask
  Death in Midsummer
Eugenio Montale, Selected Poems*
Vladimir Nabokov, Laughter in the Dark
  Nikolai Gogol
  The Real Life of Sebastian Knight
Raduan Nassar, A Cup of Rage
Pablo Neruda, The Captain's Verses*
  Love Poems*
  Residence on
Charles Olson, Selected Writings
George Oppen, New Collected Poems
Wilfred Owen, Collected Poems
Michael Palmer, The Laughter of the Sphinx
Nicanor Parra, Antipoems*
Boris Pasternak, Safe Conduct
Kenneth Patchen
  Memoirs of a Shy Pornographer
Octavio Paz, Poems of Octavio Paz
Victor Pelevin, Omon Ra
Alejandra Pizarnik
  Extracting the Stone of Madness
Ezra Pound, The Cantos
  New Selected Poems and Translations
Raymond Queneau, Exercises in Style
Qian Zhongshu, Fortress Besieged
Raja Rao, Kanthapura
Herbert Read, The Green Child
Kenneth Rexroth, Selected Poems
Keith Ridgway, Hawthorn & Child
Rainer Maria Rilke
  Poems from the Book of Hours
Arthur Rimbaud, Illuminations*
  A Season in Hell and The Drunken Boat*
Guillermo Rosales, The Halfway House
Evelio Rosero, The Armies
Fran Ross, Oreo
Joseph Roth, The Emperor's Tomb
  The Hotel Years

Raymond Roussel, Locus Solus
Ihara Saikaku, The Life of an Amorous Woman
Nathalie Sarraute, Tropisms
Jean-Paul Sartre, Nausea
  The Wall
Delmore Schwartz
  In Dreams Begin Responsibilities
Hasan Shah, The Dancing Girl
W. G. Sebald, The Emigrants
  The Rings of Saturn
  Vertigo
Stevie Smith, Best Poems
Gary Snyder, Turtle Island
Muriel Spark, The Driver's Seat
  The Girls of Slender Means
  Memento Mori
Reiner Stach, Is That Kafka?
Antonio Tabucchi, Pereira Maintains
Junichiro Tanizaki, A Cat, a Man & Two Women
Yoko Tawada, The Emissary
  Memoirs of a Polar Bear
Dylan Thomas, A Child's Christmas in Wales
  Collected Poems
Uwe Timm, The Invention of Curried Sausage
Tomas Tranströmer
  The Great Enigma: New Collected Poems
Leonid Tsypkin, Summer in Baden-Baden
Tu Fu, Selected Poems
Frederic Tuten, The Adventures of Mao
Regina Ullmann, The Country Road
Paul Valéry, Selected Writings
Enrique Vila-Matas, Bartleby & Co.
  Vampire in Love
Elio Vittorini, Conversations in Sicily
Rosmarie Waldrop, Gap Gardening
Robert Walser, The Assistant
  Microscripts
  The Tanners
Eliot Weinberger, The Ghosts of Birds
Nathanael West, The Day of the Locust
  Miss Lonelyhearts
Tennessee Williams, Cat on a Hot Tin Roof
  The Glass Menagerie
  A Streetcar Named Desire
William Carlos Williams, Selected Poems
  Spring and All
Mushtaq Ahmed Yousufi, Mirages of the Mind
Louis Zukofsky, "A"
  Anew

*BILINGUAL EDITION

For a complete listing, request a free catalog from New Directions, 80 8th Avenue, New York, NY 10011
or visit us online at ndbooks.com